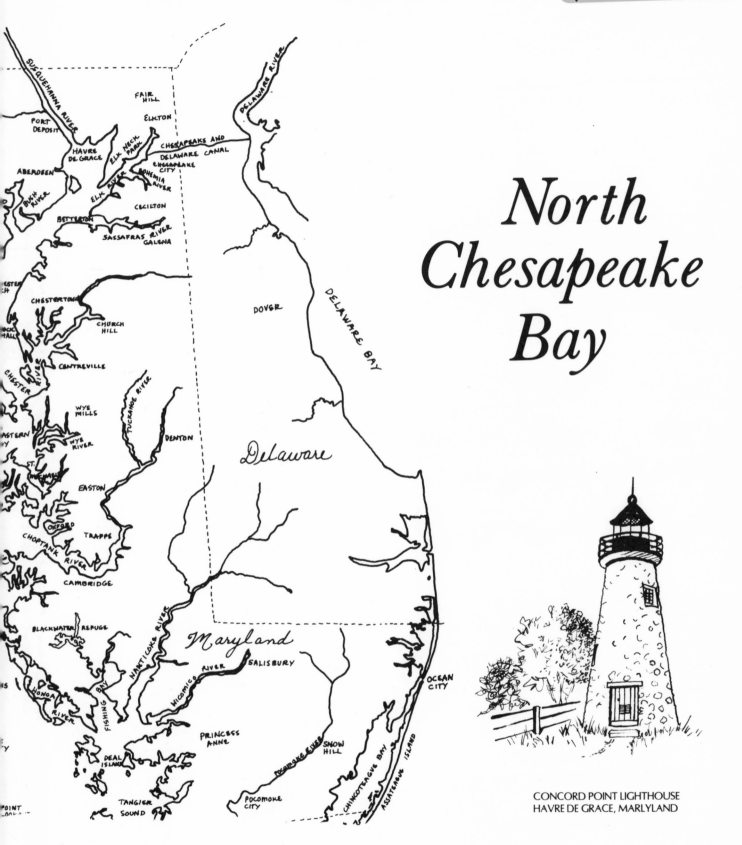

North Chesapeake Bay

CONCORD POINT LIGHTHOUSE
HAVRE DE GRACE, MARLYLAND

Illustrated by Barbara H. Hamer

FOUR SEASONS
OF THE
CHESAPEAKE BAY

This is the _4811_ copy of a limited edition of 5,000 books.

BACK END OF TOWN CREEK, OXFORD, MD

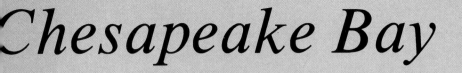

Chesapeake Bay

Red Hamer, *Author-Photographer*

Barbara H. Hamer, *Associate Editor — Illustrator*

Volume II
Fall-Winter Edition

An All-Color Pictorial of the Entire Chesapeake Bay

Printed By
Taylor Publishing Co.
Dallas, Texas; Malvern, PA

Published By
Four Seasons Book Publishers
P.O. Box 0222
West Chester, PA 19382

First Printing — November, 1982
Second Printing — September, 1984

ISBN Number 0-9605400-2-4

ACKNOWLEDGMENTS

We gratefully acknowledge the aid of the following persons in compiling this Fall-Winter color portrait of the Chesapeake Bay:

Peggy and Bart Bishop, who made their lovely Greenwood Hall Farm in Grasonville, Md. our home during the entire workup of this book: we were not always able to capture on film the running red foxes, deer, owls, hawks, eagles, heron and other wild things there, but we came to appreciate the possibilities.

Joe Bowes, Lexington Park, Md., book dealer, who pointed us in the direction of the Amish, among other people and places.

Clementine Rhodes Bowman, who tuned up our Gloucester County, Va. history.

Virginia Burton, who answered all of our questions about her beautiful town of Urbanna, Va., and the Rosewell ruins down the road.

Verdie Eberle and Paul Pallett, of Annapolis, and *Ed LaDrew* of Downington, Pa. who printed and re-printed the glossies and with great care.

Bob Fears, deputy sheriff of Northampton County, Va. who put me up and put up with me while we chased wild animals together through the marshlands and dunes of his Virginia Eastern Shore: Bob modeled as the deer hunter and as *Balboa* overlooking the Chesapeake from atop an 80-foot dune.

Page G. Hunt, owner of the Book Nook in Kilmarnock, Va. who worked so hard in putting together a book signing aboard *Casablanca* the first day of spring at the Tides Inn.

Neal Kimmel, director of the Fine Books Division, Taylor Publishing Co., who was always the perfect host and who understood that we wanted a book of enduring quality.

Capt. John Larrimore, Tilghman Island, owner of the skipjack E.C. Collier, who welcomed us aboard his working sailboat for a cold day at sea and first hand observance of the oystering industry.

Penny Lamperez and family, Paoli, Pa., for kindness to my wife, Barbara, and for all of the hours of boxing books and stapling, folding and processing flyers.

Jim and Carol Orange, for their hospitality aboard *Ebenezer II,* a 72-foot Trumpy motoryacht, and for background information on this vintage and elegant antique of the Chesapeake.

John and Heather Treanor, owners of Rolph's Wharf on the Chester River, for their hospitality at that goose hunter's paradise.

Don Walbert of Greenwood Creek, for pointing out the local bald eagle's nest that resulted in 150 photographs and a working knowledge of these macho flying machines.

Anne R. Wheeler, of Urbanna, Va., who took us on a tour of Eagle stoops on the Rappahannock River and Urbanna Creek, and to an active nest that supplied photographs for this book.

Andy Wylie, delightful owner of Irvington Marina, who took good care of our *Casablanca* over the fall, winter and spring and took us on a memorable aerial shooting spree in his pontooned *"Wild Goose."*

Contents

ADVENTURES OF AN ACCIDENT-PRONE CAMERAMAN

Three adventuresome years went into the making of *FOUR SEASONS OF THE CHESAPEAKE BAY, VOLUMES I and II*. Snowstorms, speeding tickets, a near plunge from the Woodrow Wilson Bridge in Washington, D.C.; an encounter with a marijuana yacht, a near-disastrous fall from our boat, *Casablanca;* a seven-week tug of war with my car in a frozen cornfield — These were "side car" happenings in a Keystone Kops chase of animals, people, buildings and ships.

The most memorable snowstorm occurred January 13, 1982 when I filmed the presidential yacht *Sequoia* and America's oldest warship *Constellation* in the peaceful setting of the Inner Harbor.

As it is with weather, what was a scene of tranquility in Baltimore was a stage for disaster in Washington. At 4:04 that afternoon an Air Florida 737 jet crashed into the frozen Potomac.

The picture taking on January 29 on the frozen Tred Avon River also had its mixed blessings. On this clear day I gave up a trip to Philadelphia for the "funeral" of *The Bulletin*. I had worked for that grand old newspaper as a sports writer. I re-scheduled myself to photograph hand rake tongers, waterfowl and an oyster diver. A cameraman gets only a handful of days with a negligible sun shield. This was one of those days. But I felt a deep sense of loss and I yearned to be at *The Bulletin;* it had been my family for 16 years.

The Chesapeake, whose weather patterns are notoriously erratic, produced a snowfall 150 miles south of our rented Eastern Shore farm house on Christmas Day, 1981. I thought of future Christmases I would spend with my family, and headed for "the weather." I found Quinby Harbor and Machipongo Bay all dressed up in coats of white waiting to have their picture taken.

I tried to drive quickly north the next day to my Pennsylvania homestead — where I had sent my family on Christmas Day — but, alas, gave up the project in Princess Anne, Md. where a state policeman pulled me over for speeding. Mother was not pleased. Neither was I.

Tall ships make great pictures, but tricky winds make the schedules of these magnificent sailing vessels subject to change. The photographer's game plan is to "hurry up and wait." During the "hurry up" part — quite some time before day break in the town of Denton, Md. — I received another speeding ticket. "I guess I should have stayed in bed," I said smilingly to the state trooper. He said nothing and kept writing.

This was not the day I almost fell off the Woodrow Wilson Bridge in pursuit of another tall ship. At the precise moment I was attempting to get a better camera angle on the *Danmark*, the piece of steel upon which I was standing began to pivot. I hopped quickly down to the bridge pavement as the span opened to allow the passage of this great ship.

Have you ever been a neighbor to a marijuana boat? We were. One such yacht parked next to *Casablanca* at Tolchester Marina in October, 1981. We should have been suspicious when a helicopter hovered above as the boat, *Fisherman's Paradise Too*, headed in for repairs. Who owns the 61-foot yacht, I inquired of a crewman. "Five companies," he replied. That ended the conversation. After her three-week stay at Tochester she headed south and was picked up by a Coast Guard cutter at the mouth of the Rappahannock River. She had ten tons of marijuana aboard which explains her slight list as she left Tolchester, which also explains the Coast Guard's "suspicions." It was the ninth drug bust on the Chesapeake that year.

That I fell off *Casablanca* in the summer of '81 and dislocated a shoulder had no significant relationship to the books other than if circumstances were a bit different — or had I fallen a few inches to the left or the right — there may not have been a Volume II. And this is a good lesson for every boater. Every two years we painted the deck a semigloss white. We now use a grit compound mixed in with the deck paint. It was about 8:30 at night when my smooth-soled tennis shoe came down on the dew slickened deck. I flipped 180 degrees and fell head first through a narrow opening between the boat and the dock. I grabbed a rope but discovered very quickly the left shoulder was out. Nobody was in sight or in earshot, so I swung from one rope to another with the good arm to cover the 40 or so feet to a ladder.

My car, a hatchback which carries my five-foot dinghy when necessary, also has a propensity for getting into trouble — helped somewhat by the driver. I drove the car deep into our landlady's cornfield (bog) one November day to set up a kind of blind for wild animal picture taking. After many freezes, many thaws and ten snowstorms, friendly neighbors helped to pry the car loose. One good thing came of this. I kept the poachers away. For, as one man said to me, "I didn't know that was *your* car over there. I thought it was the game warden."

Red Hamer
Greenwood Creek, Md.

NORTHWARD HO . . . *Dorothy Foster,* an oyster buy boat built in Deltaville, Va. in 1917, cruises toward Chestertown past Rolph's Wharf on the Chester River. On this day, she was leading the *Pride of Baltimore,* a 9½-foot draft clipper schooner, through the deep channel to the Kent County seat's 275th birthday celebration.

NORTH CHESAPEAKE

MISCHIEF MAKER . . . Carter Stanton tries to have a serious conversation with his hunting dog, *Tiller*, at his Chestertown farm, but the labrador retriever prefers to pull the hat over his master's ears, such is the playful disposition of the Bay 's other major hunting dog. Chesapeakes are more inclined toward business. Carter is part-owner of the *Dorothy Foster* (left page).

REMINGTON FARM's annual Hunting and Fishing Day near Rock Hall features a display of decoys and firearms among other exhibits and activities.

THE HUNTING SCENARIO (left) began one late October day at Rolph's Wharf on the Chester River. Scott Livie, of Chestertown, was laying out his decoys when he spied a "live one" coming in to join the party. What a spot without a shot gun! Scott returned to his blind to let loose with a few goose calls while his faithful Chesapeake retriever *BOOZER* scoured the sky. *BOOZER* got his name by stealing his master's scotch and soda as a puppy. When Scott got his goose, *BOOZER* went into action (near left). "I saw him swim 100 yards for a bird, and return, and not even seem winded," said Livie, who organizes hunting parties in the Chestertown area. The Chester River is one of the best goose hunting areas on the entire Bay.

CHESTER RIVER LANDMARKS . . . Kennersley (top), grand old (1705) farm plantation situated on Island Creek just off the eastern side of the upper Chester River from which nearby Kennersley Pointe Marina takes its name. The Inn at Rolph's Wharf (right) goes back to 1830. Steamboats came to its wharf at the turn of the century to pick up farm produce. Passengers also boarded here on the Baltimore to Chestertown route.

CENTREVILLE . . . the county seat of Queen Anne's County, is a living museum in many respects. At top is Wright's Chance, home of the county's historical society. The manor house dates to 1744 and was rescued and moved from a nearby farm where it was about to be demolished. Four beautifully panelled rooms were uncovered under plaster during restoration. At left, St.Paul's Parish, on Liberty Street, founded in 1640. The first church was built in the late 1600s, and rebuilt a number of times. The communion silver still in use is dated 1717. At right is historic Lawyers Row.

PEACE AND PLENTY . . .Centreville landmark at the corner of Routes 301 and 213; believed to have been built in 1774. The brick building of a late Georgian and early Federal style was owned, until recent years, by Mrs. Dorothy Wright, a descendant of the family that owned Wright's Chance, now the home of the Queen Anne's County Historical Society.

CHESTERTOWN

DOUBLE CELEBRATION . . . Chestertown toasted its 275th year of existence in 1981 and the 200th birthday of Washington College. Carriages with Clydesdale horses carried dignitaries past the Kent County seat's architectural monuments: the Pinder Building (above), Hynson-Ringgold House, circa 1735, (left); and Swan Tavern, (below). During a recent archeological dig, a well predating 1700 was discovered on the tavern property along with coins dating to the 1680s. WASHINGTON COLLEGE (right page): framed by the musty attic window of the Dunning Science Building.

Top: **CHESTERTOWN SHOWPLACE . . .** This beautiful waterfront home, *Widehall,* was built in 1762 by Thomas Smyth, the wealthiest merchant in the busiest port of the Eastern Shore. Two U.S. Senators also lived here — Robert Wright (governor of Maryland 1806-09) and Ezekial F. Chambers. Below: **CANADIAN GEESE** huddle on the Chester River ice on the western shore of Chestertown above the bridge that connects Kent and Queen Anne's counties.

PRIDE OF BALTIMORE . . . at anchor in Chestertown. Baltimore's goodwill ambassador, which logged nearly 30,000 miles her first two years, is a composite of the rakish Baltimore clippers of the early 1800s — except she has better wood. For example, the keel of this 137-foot long ship was fashioned from lignum vitae over 1,000 years old. 18th and early 19th century construction methods were used as the boat was built in 10 months in Baltimore's Inner Harbor. She was finished in 1977. She is the first ship of her class to be built in more than 100 years.

WESLEY CHAPEL (circa 1852) . . .
Rock Hall, Md. (left page)

TOLCHESTER MARINA . . . Refuge and stopover point for pleasure and workboats in the upper Bay. From its entrance light (right) to Baltimore — some 20 miles across the bay — ice more than a foot thick brought marine travel to a halt in January, 1982. Tolchester was named after William Tolson, one of Kent County's earliest settlers, who had his grant surveyed in 1672. Nearby are ancient St. Paul's Church (circa 1711), the quaint fishing village of Rock Hall, and the charming, colonial town of Chestertown. The British stormed Tolchester in 1814 and were defeated in the battle of nearby Caulk's Field. Tolchester Beach was a popular bay resort in the 1920s and 1930s when excursion steamers brought city dwellers across the Bay.

18

SASSAFRAS RIVER . . . Capt. John Smith and his band of consummate adventurers explored this lovely river in 1607-09 and a monument testifies to that fact on the right hand side of the Route 213 bridge. The Georgetown Yacht Basin (extreme left), the Sassafras Boat Co. (to the immediate left and right of the bridge) and several other marinas make this one of the major yachting centers of the upper Eastern Shore. This ten-mile fetch from the bridge to the Bay is replete with gunkholes and sandy beaches. Devoid of sea nettles, the Sassafras has been one

SWAN CREEK MARINA . . . A sustained thaw was nine days old when this photograph was made, but this Rock Hall, Maryland marina was still locked in as well as the entire Sassafras River (above) in February, 1982.

Top: **SNOW BLOWER** . . . One pickup truck fights the blowing snow on Route 213 between the Bohemia River and Chesapeake and Delaware Canal. Bottom: **THE ANCHORAGE** . . . Home of the Lusbys in the early 1700s, this landmark is a becoming retreat to colonial times as one enters Cecilton from the East on Route 213. The marker reads: "Ruth Lusby and Commodore Jacob Jones married in 1821, made *Anchorage* their home and enlarged it in 1835. Jones served on the *Philadelphia* when it ran aground at Tripoli and commanded the sloop *Wasp* during the War of 1812.

NEEDLES . . . Setting sun turns all sailboat masts into glowing needles at Georgetown Yacht Basin on the upper Sassafras. This picture was made on the back lawn of the historic Kitty Knight House.

CHESAPEAKE AND DELAWARE CANAL ... Cargo ship from Bombay, India (above) emerges from under the 135-foot high Chesapeake City Bridge and takes Schaefer's Dock and Canal House Restaurant on its port as it heads to the Delaware River 15 miles away. Pilot boat (right) speeds through the ice, pulls alongside the freighter, the pilot captain climbs a rope ladder to deliver a packet of orders, then descends to the smaller boat and pulls away ... all while the freighter maintains its speed through the canal. Three miles is required for a ship of this magnitude to stop. Below, water level view of the bridge, and Schaefer's. The canal was dug by hand starting in 1814, but was not navigable until 1849. In 1972 the canal was cut to a depth of 35 feet and a width of 450 feet. Six bridges traverse it, including a railroad lift span which a freighter crashed into in 1973 when the automatic lift failed to operate. The canal and bridge were closed to traffic for months.

ICE FISHING ON THE NORTH EAST RIVER . . . On this very spot (above) is held the North East River Festival with water acrobats, kite skiing and boat races — but that's another season. Herb Benjamin, of Herb's Tackle Shop in downtown North East, and son Mike, 13, take advantage of the January freeze of '82 that turned the Bay into a tundra from the two bridges to North East. Pickings are slim, with only a mud shad, rock fish and white perch to show for their vigil. Herb keeps warm wrapped in an all-leather World War II flying suit he bought for $18.

CHARLIE THE GOOSE . . . 12-year-old mascot of McDaniel's Yacht Basin, North East River. Charlie recently was memorialized before his time in an oil painting. Charlie keeps the ducks in line at the popular yachting center.

BOHEMIA MANOR . . . From this elevation is one of the more imposing views of the scenic Bohemia River. This manor house was built in 1920 by U.S. Senator Thomas Bayard, of Delaware, a direct descendant of Augustine Herrman, the famous mapmaker. Herrman was born in Prague, Bohemia in 1605. He sailed to America in 1633 and spent 10 years drawing an astonishingly accurate map of the Chesapeake Bay. For this feat Lord Baltimore awarded him vast land holdings in the "farr remote unknown wilderness" of the Bay which he named Bohemia Manor. Herrman built two manor houses, the first in 1676, but they burned down. Owner of the third manor is James A. Bayard, son of the late senator. Etched on concrete markers between the second story windows are the initials of Augustine and Jannetae Herrman (1660) and Thomas and Elizabeth Bayard (1920).

GREAT HOUSE . . . located on the shores of the upper Bohemia. The main part was constructed in the 1750s, the smaller part about 1650, making it one of the oldest houses on the Bay. It is known that the short-lived Labadist religious sect built a structure known as *Great House* in the 17th century. The estate, which has interesting animals such as the llama (left) is owned by the Richard duPonts, Jr.

HISTORIC CORNER . . . St. Augustine Church (left), erected in 1838 and completely restored in 1963. From the backyard cemetery (above) the eye is confronted with a magnificent 200-year-old Georgian colonial, in the hamlet of Augustine, where race horses are bred.

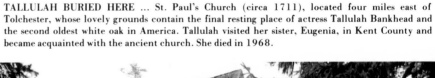

TALLULAH BURIED HERE ... St. Paul's Church (circa 1711), located four miles east of Tolchester, whose lovely grounds contain the final resting place of actress Tallulah Bankhead and the second oldest white oak in America. Tallulah visited her sister, Eugenia, in Kent County and became acquainted with the ancient church. She died in 1968.

HAVRE DE GRACE . . . boating town where the Susquehanna meets the Chesapeake, burned to the ground by the infamous British Admiral Cockburn in 1813. Old Concord Point Lighthouse (above) operated from 1829 to 1976, once the oldest continually used lighthouse on the East Coast; Havre de Grace Marina on Water St., (left) and a pair of sailboats that chose to remain out of drydock a bit longer, against the backdrop of the Susquehanna River railroad bridge.

RODGERS TAVERN . . . (right), Perryville, Md. Named in memory of Col. John Rodgers (1726-1791), patriot, inn keeper and friend of George Washington, who dined here April, May and September, 1775. The restored tavern, built in the 1700s, served the needs of those using the ferry on the Susquehanna River (shown to the left of building). The Lower Susquehanna ferry was established in 1695. The old post road in front of Rodgers Tavern was carved out in 1666.

EARLY WATER TOWER . . . Historic Charlestown, Maryland, on the North East River.

FAIR HILL INN (below) . . . circa 1764, located in hunt country to the west of Elkton. It served as summer and retirement home of Dr. Abraham Mitchell, who tended the Continental troops at his Elkton home during the Revolution.

DAFFODILS wished they had stayed in bed as late winter storm brushed this cluster of old stone buildings in Fair Hill, Md. Known as the Bee Hive, the buildings — on Route 273 — were used to build farm implements and to house farm supplies. One was a tavern.

IT'S NOT PURE CORN . . . Swans *can* be friendly, especially in Oxford, Md. (right) Just in case, bring food. Oldest privately owned ferry boat service in America ties up here. But not always in January, when this picture was made.

UPPER
EASTERN SHORE

EARECKSON HOMESTEAD, circa 1856 or older, sits on the highest ground on old Kent Island, 19 feet above sea level, in the afternoon shadow of the twin Chesapeake Bay bridges. This is the sole remaining structure of the original Broad Creek Plantation which dates to 1650, some 19 years after Kent Island accepted its first white settler. The house has an exquisite winding open string staircase. Kitty Rose, an structure is used for commercial offices today, including yacht sales. J. Leif Eareckson, of Troy, Mich., stated in a 1973 letter to Mrs. Rose that "I am under the impression that the walls were raised in 1792, probably by Charles Eareckson, who . . . was commissioned an ensign in the 20th Battalion of Militia, Queen Anne's County" during the Revolution.

CRUSHED ICE IN FANCY COLORS is the Chesapeake Bay offering in this wintry, twilight scene setting off the twin Chesapeake Bay bridges connecting Kent Island (foreground) of the Eastern Shore with Sandy Point of the western shore, 4.3 miles distant. One bridge was completed in 1952, the other in 1964.

HARVEST TIME . . . The two major farm crops in Queen Anne's County are soy beans and corn, and the migrating Canadian geese are glad that the choice here at Greenwood Hall Farm is the latter. The leavings won't be turned under until spring. Greenwood Creek is in background.

PUMPKINS GALORE at Bennett Point General Store. And Rudy the cat (left) will make sure you don't steal one. Jim Knight has everything for the country bumpkin at his colorful Queen Anne's County store located at Bryantown Landing on the Wye River — crab pots, crab seasoning and crabs, vegetables and fruits right off the local farms, fresh meats, wood stoves, antiques and a forest of chrysanthemums for Rudy to hide under.

OBJETS D'ART . . . Frozen stiff on a day when temperatures plunged below zero in 33 of the 48 continental states making it "the coldest day of the century;" Cabin Creek, Grasonville, January 11, 1982.

TRANQUILITY comes in many seasons, but seldom so esthetically as in autumn when decoys float in the glow of a sunset: Greenwood Hall Farm, Greenwood Creek.

PROSPECT BAY LIGHTHOUSE is nouveau built and takes its name from the waters which lead into Kent Narrows. It is not a beacon for ships, but an esthetic keynote to a combination golf and country club and home development in Queen Anne's County. Deer, fox and a bald eagle family reside on these waterside acres, a blueprint for blending civilization with the wild and the free.

RUNNING WILD in a sanctuary of rolling hills, forests and regular feedings is this herd of fallow (white) deer and "friends" at Wye Heights Plantation on the Wye River. Fallow deer were brought down from the Catskill Game Preserve in New York. They are European in origin. "Wild" deer find the fallow deer's turf so attractive they jump the fences to get in.

SMALL STREAMS provide the real beauty of the Chesapeake Bay. Left, Easton Point on the frozen Tred Avon River, where otters can sometimes be seen at play in early morning, sliding across the ice; Top, Greenwood Creek, where oyster tongers are observed from the banks of Greenwood Hall Farm; and below, Bryantown Landing, on the upper Wye River.

OLD WYE OAK, once the property of Wye Landing Farm (right page), was burdened with 10 snowfalls during the winter of 1981-82, but came out blooming in the late spring. Maryland's state tree is extremely well cared for which explains why it is America's oldest (440 years) and largest white oak. It sits across from a granary on the Talbot County side of Wye Mills.

WYE RIVER HISTORY . . . Some of the richest documented American history lies in and around the tiny town of Wye Mills just off Route 50 and the East Wye River. On the Queen Anne's County side of the town is Wye Mill (right), in operation since 1671. The mill still produces highly prized ground cornmeal, just as it did for Washington's army in 1778; white, whole wheat, rye and buckwheat flour. The **LITTLE RED SCHOOLHOUSE** (below) is the only one-room schoolhouse remaining in Talbot County. It was built in 1885 in Longwoods. **WYE LANDING FARM,** bottom, looks down on the Wye River from its high perch. This was once the manor house for one of the largest plantations in Talbot County, exceeding 4,000 acres and worked by 79 slaves. The kitchen wing was originally built in 1698 and served as the main house.

TALBOT COUNTY COURT HOUSE (above) . . . When the first court house went up on this site in 1711, it was only the second building in Easton. The first town dwelling was the wood frame Third Haven Meeting House (1684), but that was located some distance away on a spot where the Tred Avon River almost joined the Miles. The main section of this present court house was built in 1794.

CAROLINE COUNTY'S first court house was built on its present site in Denton in 1797. The green, referred to then as Pig Point, was purchased in 1791 for 120 shillings. Last renovations and additions to the court house were in 1966. Christ Episcopal Church can be seen behind the court house. Behind the church is the Choptank River.

SCRATCHING FOR A LIVING . . . Canadian geese set up shop on this snowy farm field on the bypass across from Tred Avon Square, Easton. No dumb "animals," geese establish sentinels along the perimeter of their flock. The Canada goose formerly migrated heavily into North Carolina, but Eastern Shore farmers are growing more corn and the mechanical corn pickers leave a lot behind for the incoming geese. They plow it under in the fall in North Carolina; not until spring on the Eastern Shore.

TALBOT COUNTY CHAMBER OF COMMERCE lives (left) on Route 50 in the transplanted home of an early ship builder, Capt. Clement Vickers. House is known as Tilghman's Fortune.

VIBRANT FOLIAGE . . . Autumn's colors reach their peak in Easton the last half of October. This photograph was made October 25. The friendly open doors belong to the SS Peter and Paul Catholic Church on Goldsborough Street.

THE BULLITT HOUSE . . . From an archway of the Tidewater Inn (above) on Dover Street, Easton, can be seen the Federal styling of the Bullitt House (right page) which was completed in 1801. The inn, constructed in 1949, and the Bullitt House help to set the architectural character of "the colonial capital of Maryland's Eastern Shore." Bullitt, a young lawyer from Virginia, oversaw the construction of his superb home for three years before moving in. It was said that he was the last gentleman to walk the streets of Easton dressed in colonial garb — knee britches, swallow tailed coat and silver buckles on his shoes. The Walsh and Benson real estate firm now occupies the building. The 200-room Tidewater Inn serves as headquarters for the annual Waterfowl Festival in November and bills itself as "the pride of the Eastern Shore."

44

Above: **NO, THIS IS NOT A HUDSON BAY OUTPOST** but the boat building shop at the Chesapeake Bay Maritime Museum, St. Michael's. The near water is kept unfrozen by a bubbler system.

Above, left page: **CHRISTMAS AT LONGFELLOW'S RESTAURANT**, St. Michael's Harbor. Below, **CHRISTMAS SKIPJACK** at Applegarth's Boatyard, Town Creek, Oxford. Bob Cain, of Media, Pa., supplies the boat, Applegarth's rigs up the lights and the town pays the electric bill. "Everybody looks forward to seeing the Christmas boat lights go on December 15," said Mr. Applegarth.

SPY HOUSE AND CLIPPER SHIPS . . . Thomas Kemp, who bought Wade Point Farm (middle) in 1813 while he was constructing clipper ships in nearby St. Michaels Harbor, used a very powerful spy glass to keep an eye out for ships that he owned coming up the Eastern Bay. He did his spying from the chimney (left) or "spy house." Kemp was born at Bolton Farm (below), then called the Quaker Kemp Place, which is a few miles south of Wade Point on the way to Tilghman Island. Mildred Kemp, 88, who related this information, is the seventh generation of the Quaker family to live at Wade Point. Mildred was a Tunis (Tunis Mills was named after her uncle). Her father, Henry Clay Tunis, was born in Fairview, which today is Longfellows Restaurant in St. Michaels Harbor. The original Wade Point Farm, named after Zachary Wade who obtained a grant from the king of England in 1657, "may have been built out in the bay" on land now under water, according to Mildred.

THE INN AT PERRY CABIN, St. Michaels, Md., is one of the showplace restaurant-inns of the Chesapeake Bay. The panoramic windows and Jeffersonian pillars of this handsomely rebuilt cupola-topped entertainment center look out on a scene of workboats and pleasure boats plying the historic Miles River. Hordes of Canadian geese entertain customers in the fall and winter. The structure was known as Perry Cabin when it was a plantation in the early 1700s. It later became a lodge but it was not known as The Inn at Perry Cabin until the Meyerhoff family bought the property and rebuilt the old structure in 1980. The Meyerhoffs are better known as owners of Spectacular Bid when he won the Kentucky Derby and

Preakness in 1979 and eventually became the biggest money winning horse of all time before retiring to stud. Samuel Hambleton and Frederick Douglass lived on the premises under different circumstances in the 1800s. Hambleton, who served under Commodore Perry in the War of 1812, lived in the main house. Douglass, who later became U.S. Minister to Haiti, lived here in a shack between 1833 and 1836 — as a slave. He taught himself to read and write and conducted a clandestine school for blacks before escaping north to become a noted abolitionist, orator and editor. In recent years, Jim Thomas, a distant Douglass relative, became town commission president of St. Michaels.

CAPT. JOHN LARRIMORE (right) edges his *E.C. Collier* onto an oyster hill by checking the depth finder. "We'll be cruising along at 20 feet and suddenly it's 16. That's a hill." His skipjack was built on Deal Island in 1910. John Cummings, his son in law and captain; Larrimore and a crew of four head out of Dogwood Harbor at 6 a.m. every day except Sunday in search of their daily limit of 150 bushels. A crew member can make as much as $1500 some weeks "but they work in God awful weather," cautions the 73-year-old owner. Icicles were hanging off the tender (push boat) most of this March 20th, and snow flurries constantly swept across the broad, choppy Choptank. "I'd rather go out in December than March," said Larrimore. "This has been the worst week of the season."

Larrimore, whose ancestors settled in the area in 1662, never finished high school, but he founded a course in marine science at Chesapeake College where he has taught for 10 years. "If you can't learn something in 50 years out here," he said, "you never will."

CREW pulls aboard dredger full of oysters (right) and sorts out the good from the bad. The bivalves get a good washing down (above) enroute home to Tilghman Island.

HEADING HOME . . . Four of Tilghman Island's 13 skipjacks head home after a long day on the Choptank. Skipjacks are America's last working sailboats.

SUNRISE AT DOGWOOD HARBOR . . . Skipjacks line up at one of Tilghman Island's two main harbors before their daily plunge into the Choptank. The last of America's working sailboats have long histories — some fraught with tragedy. The Claude W. Somers, whose transom is partially visible, was constructed in 1908 in Oriole, Maryland. She has lost two crews to the often frigid waters of the Chesapeake — the first time in 1920 and again in 1976 during a winter gale.

MASTER SHIPWRIGHT James Byron Richardson surveys his frozen boat yard in Lloyds, Maryland on LeCompte Creek while a carpenter puts the finishing touches on the oyster buy boat, MISTER JIM, named after the LeCompte Creek "philosopher." "LeCompte came here in 1650," Richardson said. "They tell me the creek was vastly different then, at least four feet deeper. Since then the farmers have been plowing close to the water and heavy rains have washed the soil into the water basins . . . The forest was full of oak then, not a lot of this underbrush. I think the settlers brought that with them. I would like to have seen the creek then, but if I did I wouldn't know anything about space travel, would I? . . . We have Indian burial grounds here. They buried their women and children in one place, their men in another. According to the bones I saw, the men were as big as me — six feet, I was once. My father ran a sewer from the house to the creek and he came across a skeleton chest high. But he would not let us kids play with that skeleton. His very words were, 'We ought to have respect for the dead.' . . . The Chryslers over there (who lived at Pokety Farm, across the creek) saved many nail kegs full of Indian skeletons when Mr. Chrysler was enlarging the cellar. Their teeth were reasonably good, but their joints were swollen with arthritis. They had to go barefoot to get their oysters in the winter."

LeCompte Creek Philosopher

"Two Indian canoes were dug up in the Cambridge Creek when they were dredging it in 1900. But we have some turning up in marshes yet — enough so that we know they were crude. They resembled swine troughs, as John Smith used to say. I had a feeling that Smith looked at Indian canoes like I look at the metric system, but when I saw the canoes myself I found he was right. Some of the people of this immediate neighborhood hold Captain Smith in rather low repute because he missed the Choptank completely (in his historic 1608 exploration of the Bay). But we suspected how he missed it. The mouth of it looked so much like the Bay."

FOGGY MORNING IN OXFORD . . . Putt, putt, putt is a familiar sound at the crack of dawn — even a foggy dawn — as the crab fleet heads out of Town Creek. This picture was made at Bates Marina looking across at Cutts and Case ship yard.

"I GUESS THE INDIANS DID THIS, except they didn't stay down so long," joked oyster diver Mike Harrison (above), who worked under the ice of Oxford's Tred Avon River in two-hour shifts on January 29, 1982. Buoyed with air hose, rope and hot water hose to keep his $250 rubber suit toasty warm, Mike came up with a harvest. "It takes three years to grow an oyster," he said. "These are six to seven years old. They die when they get this big . . . from old age." Harrison works under the water in the summer cleaning boats, but makes most of his money diving for oysters — not always in these conditions. "We couldn't take a chance on taking all of this equipment on the ice last year," said Mike. "It was only four inches thick." That's a bit risky for a human being, too. Closer to land, two dogs play along the frozen pilings of Oxford, their designs carved by the tides.

55

TAKING OYSTERS OUT OF THE DEEP FREEZE . . . That's what James (Peewee) Lempke called this hand tonging operation on the Tred Avon River during one of the coldest winters on record in 1982. Peewee, sorting out the bivales (left page) with his Trappe neighbor Donald Haddaway (with tongs), added: "This work takes a strong back and a weak mind." They hauled up nine bushels this January 29, the last day before a sustained thaw. They had been working the ice, some areas as thick as 15 inches, for two weeks. They cut the ice with buck and power saws and sometimes used an axe. The toughest part was hauling the loaded baskets by sled to the pickup truck near the Tred Avon Yacht Club at the northwest end of Oxford. "We were both born and raised in Oxford when it was a waterman's town," said Peewee. "But we can't afford it anymore. It's a millionaires' town now." Across the frozen tundra is Benoni Point where the Susquehannocks came down to wipe out the local Indian tribe in the 1600s.

ON THE FLY . . . Favorite gathering place for waterfowl in Oxford where The Strand meets the Robert Morris Inn. These ducks and swan don't migrate because residents and tourists insist on feeding them their daily corn.

BLACKWATER REFUGE — west of Cambridge, Md. — where 100,000 Canada geese migrate every autumn from Ungava, land of Cree Indians and Eskimos between the James and Hudson Bays. Blackwater's 11,000 acres were established as a wildlife refuge in 1933. Left, **WANTED: SCHOOL CROSSING GUARD.**

FRIENDSHIP HALL (above) . . . located just south of Cambridge in East New Market which has been the center for Methodism for more than 200 years. The three-story brick plantation house was built about 1740 and was the home of the Sullivane family, three generations of whom served in the Maryland General Assembly.

FARMS AND THEIR CEMETERIES . . . While weekend motorists using Route 50 enroute to Ocean City have visions of sandy beaches in their minds, the visions seen by their eyes are of farms. The crisply neat farm above is north of Trappe. The farm cemetery — one old marker dates to 1853 — is located between Cambridge and Salisbury. The trees are loblolly pines, often used as pilings and telephone poles, when cut.

HALF A FOOT OF NEW SNOW lends a fresh look to two Salisbury landmarks — Holloway Hall at Salisbury State College, founded in 1925, and the Zoological Park where mama llama and child find the white stuff exhilarating.

QUINBY HARBOR (left page), on the sea side of southern Accomack County, as she looked Christmas Day 1981 with a halo over her crab and oyster shacks. It had been 35 years since the lower Delmarva Peninsula woke up to snow on Christmas. Although it snowed all day, it amounted to no more than an inch.

BROWNSVILLE . . . (below), ancestral home of the distinguished Upshurs, who produced a Secretary of State in the President Zachery Taylor administration, located three miles east of Nassawadox, Virginia. In 1652 John Brown patented the land, which looks out on the bays and marshes of the barrier islands. Brown's grand-daughter married Arthur Upshur II about 1690. Caster beans were grown on the farm and pressed into caster oil. Salt was also manufactured on the property. The present brick house, with 21 inch walls, was built in 1806. The frame structures followed in 1809. The architectural plan of big house, little house, storehouse, kitchen and other dependencies was predominant in its day.

WICOMICO HUNT

The fox hunt at Salisbury, Maryland is held the first Sunday after Thanksgiving. It begins with the Blessing of the Hounds at Fox Farm (right) and ends with running a fox up a tree (below). In between, the trail runs past Pemberton Hall (left and right photos) and some watch the drama all bundled up in a carriage. Pemberton Hall was built in 1741 by Col. Isaac Handy, the same man who established a wharf and a lumber business at the head of the Wicomico in 1732 and called it Salisbury.

SNOW HILL . . . Two landmarks in this crisply neat Maryland Eastern Shore town are the All Hallows Church (above), whose parish was established in 1692 (the present brick building dates from 1748) and the Victorian style Worcester County Court House.

SUNSET BRIDGE . . . From the span that carries vehicles from Chincoteague Island to eastern Assateague Island, there is almost always a sunset . . . and lots of ducks. (facing page).

AN ARTIST AND HIS FRIENDS ... Eastern Shore artist Jack R. Schroeder, twice a winner of the Maryland waterfowl stamp contest, shows off his latest limited edition print "Not Yet!" to a feline admirer. Schroeder lives in Still Pond but was photographed above at reknown carver Lem

Ward's work shed in Crisfield while painting his feathered and furry friends such as the snow geese and fawn, filmed on Assateague Island, and young retrievers, one of which belongs to Jack's daughter.

ASSATEAGUE LIGHT . . . 142 foot high brick tower was built in 1857. Bricks were brought in by boat and hauled to the top of a sand ridge in carts pulled by oxen. Picture was made November 29 in the middle of the snow geese migratory season.

CLAMMING VESSELS at Chincoteague Bay Bridge, Chincoteague. Each has a capacity of 1,800 bushels, but they rarely catch that many since government limits each boat to 24 hours of daylight clamming per week. Before the Fisheries Management Act was passed, the industry was rapidly outcatching the resource. Now that clams are more abundant, the industry looks forward to fewer restrictions. The boats, owned by the American Original Co., run as far north as Martha's Vineyard, as far south as Cape Hatteras. Sometimes they run into foul weather as when the 90-foot *MARBLEHEAD* went down off Ocean City, Maryland, December, 1981.

THE LAST CRAB BOAT IN . . . Crab Alley, Crisfield, Maryland

LEM WARD COUNTRY . . . setting sun and snow complement one another at Crisfield's Somers Cove Harbor (above) and among its crab houses. The February storm dumped nearly 10 inches of snow here, but only rain on Cape Charles 50 miles to the south as the sea gulls fly. Lem Ward spent much of his lifetime around the crab house area — fishing, crabbing, hunting and doing what made him famous — carving decoys.

CRYSTAL PALACE lives up to its name on this snowy January morning. The Federalist style townhouse in tiny Franktown, Va. in Northampton County was constructed in 1849-50 from bricks made on the estate by the owner. Judge Charles Magruder Langford, Jr. lived here until his recent death. Route 13 is named after him. Franktown got its name from Frank Andrews who opened a store there in 1764.

73

LOVE TRIANGLE . . . Kendall Grove (circa 1790) and its striking dependencies — set off by the presence of "Patches" — bear a legend worthy of a soap opera. It seems that young George Kendall was engaged to marry Margaret Eyre when he contracted a fever in December, 1784, and died. Out of his great love for Margaret (daughter of Severn Eyre, of Eyre Hall) he willed her his land. Margaret later married George Parker, Kendall's good friend, and they built the plantation house on Kendall's land. They named it in honor of Kendall whose grave is in the burial ground to the rear of the house. The marker bears the legend "by his friend George Parker," in addition to name and dates. The dependencies (clockwise) include a kitchen with massive fireplace, dairy, store house and smoke house. The window view is from the front porch. Also shown, the house from a distance and the main porch close up. Kendall Grove is at the head of the Assawaman Creek which joins Hungars Creek before flowing into the Chesapeake just north of Eastville. The house is presently owned by the Claude A. Turners, Jr.

HAPPY UNION . . . A handsome 18th century brick house with an intriguing name, set upon a lovely lawn that runs gently down to the scenic Nassawadox Creek. The French doors (separate photo) with the arched lintel are on the left side of the house and overlook the creek . . . CLUSTER of three houses at right served as dormitories for the poor in the 1931 Depression. The Almshouse Property, as it is known, is located north of Eastville, the Northampton County seat. The brick house is a quarter kitchen constructed in the late 1600s, making it one of the oldest buildings on the Eastern Shore.

WILD AND UNTAMED . . . is the way it is in coastal sections of the Lower Delmarva Peninsula. A full antlered buck deer romps through the surf of Magotha Bay near the quaint fishing village of Oyster, Virginia on the sea side of Route 13. Over on the Chesapeake Bay side at Cherrystone Inlet — about four miles to the west — a crab basket and platform rig wash ashore among deer tracks and shadowy sand fences.

OPEN SEAS of the Virginia Eastern Shore are reflected at Sand Hill (far left), Bill Sturgis' farm on the Bay at Savage Neck where the wind-whipped dunes reach 80 feet, the highest point on the lower Delmarva Peninsula; Kiptopeke at Fisherman's Inlet (above left), the stepping off place of the 17.6 mile Chesapeake Bay Bridge and Tunnel which runs to Virginia Beach; and at Point Farm on Savage Neck (above) where the deer hunter's silhouette contrasts with the early morning blue of the Bay.

EYRE, soulful looking Chesapeake Bay retriever, romps out of the surf of Cherrystone Creek at Savage Neck on Virginia's Eastern Shore. This breed of dog native to the United States resulted from mating a Newfoundland hound and a river otter . . . if you believe Eastern Shore stories.

POINT FARM, shown at daybreak (below) and in mid-afternoon, is one of the oldest houses on the Shore. It was near here at Savage Neck that Ensign Thomas Savage landed in 1619. Savage endeared himself to the Gingaskin Indians by learning their language. Debedeavon, "laughing king" of the Indians, granted him a tract of land and he thus became the first permanent English settler on the Virginia Eastern Shore. Point Farm was built in 1725, has changed hands seven times and is presently owned by George Ames. It was restored in 1935 by Evelyn Willing of the Chestnut Hill section of Philadelphia. It is located on the Cherrystone Creek near the town of Cheriton.

HALLWAY of the main house.

PEACE ON EARTH . . . the Machipongo River on Christmas Day, 1981, on the road to Quinby Harbor. Opposite page: **ROBERTSON WINDMILL** on a late October afternoon, Williamsburg, Virginia.

LOWER WESTERN SHORE

LIAMSBURG

RESTORATION OF COLONIAL WILLIAMSBURG began more than 50 years ago, and old man winter adds a becoming January mantle. The snowy winter of 1981-82 produced the first white Christmas in Williamsburg in 35 years. From left, clockwise: the Bruton Parish Church, in continuous service since it was built in 1715; Custis-Maupin House with its Gambrels roof and massive chimneys; the store fronts of historic Duke of Gloucester Street: Scribner Book Store, The Pewter Shop, The Toymaker of Williamsburg and the Christmas Shop; Toymaker Shop, with "restored" colonial snow man; and Christiana-Campbell's Tavern, all icicles in place.

THE FORTNIGHT OF CHRISTMAS begins in Williamsburg with
the lighting of the candles in the windows of the Governor's Palace.

BERKELEY MANSION . . . birthplace of President William Henry Harrison and ancestral home of President Benjamin Harrison. This beautifully restored brick home (right page, middle photo with fireplace) was begun in 1726. It is situated in Charles City County on the James River on whose banks was celebrated the first Thanksgiving in America. This 1619 event is annually re-enacted (as shown) and was officially authenticated in 1963 by President Kennedy. Guest house (with green shutters) was built 100 years after the main house. Capt. John Woodlief and his small group of settlers arrived here aboard the **Margaret** on Dec. 4, 1619. On March 22, 1622 the entire colony at Berkeley was wiped out in an Indian uprising. The plantation is noted as the site of America's first commercial shipyard and first distillation of American bourbon whiskey. Brewmaster George Thorpe, Episcopal preacher, wrote: "A brew of corn and maize was made and was much better than British ale. The people over here were not sick in body but sick in mind and two drinks a day of this fiery water made things all right." On these lawns the entire 140,000 man Army of the Potomac encamped July and August 1862. **Taps** was composed and premiered here by Gen. William Butterfield.

SHERWOOD FOREST
. . . President John Tyler purchased the Charles City home above in 1842 and retired to it in 1845. The longest house in Virginia, its wings and connected dependencies extend 300 feet.

RICHMOND

RICHMOND . . . the capital of Virginia was laid out in 1737 and has grown to become the business and educational center of the South. The tobacco industry is king in this city of 500,000 along the James River. This photograph was made November, 1981. At left, the Confederate Soldiers and Sailors Monument at Pear and East Main Streets.

HISTORIC JAMES RIVER, 75 miles from its mouth, dwarfs these canoeists against the maze of useful and useless bridges and industrial skyline of Richmond, Virginia.

DOROTHY . . . This 90 foot, iron tugboat was the first vessel constructed by Newport News Shipbuilding and Drydock Co., the largest shipbuilding company in the world. She was launched in 1891 and a collision in 1964 ended her career. On June 19, 1975 Dorothy was restored and dedicated "to the pride and craftsmanship of the men and women of Newport News Shipbuilding." She sits on display across the street from the entrance of that company.

MOBIL TANKER rides over Thimble Shoals, one of the two tunnels of the Chesapeake Bay Bridge and Tunnel which connects Virginia Beach with the Eastern Shore. The 17.5 mile bridge-tunnel was built at a cost of $200,000,000.

THE RUINS OF ROSEWELL . . . The preservation society for this once magnificent Tidewater Virginia mansion along the York River has neatly stacked loose bricks strewn by the destructive fire of 1916. Steel girders have been installed to keep the remaining walls upright. Begun in the 1720s, the Georgian style house was unusually large, even for those times. It included an 810-square foot main hall, 23 rooms and 17 fireplaces. Mann Page I completed the house in 1744 for his wife, the daughter of the extremely wealthy King Carter. Ac-comodating his wife with a style to which she was accustomed placed great financial strain on Page's family to maintain the house. John Page, grandson of Mann I, became governor of Virginia. His lifelong friend, Thomas Jefferson, reportedly wrote the first draft of the Declaration of Independence here. HAYNES MILL POND (below) attracted a grain mill which likely served the nearby Burwell and Rosewell estates. The pond and old mill are located in Gloucester County along route 614.

CHRISTOPHER NEWPORT COLLEGE ... Autumn arrives late in Newport News and so on this November 19 there remained enough foliage to light up the campus. Above, Ratcliffe Gym. Below, main walkway through this modern institution named after the leader of that band of settlers who set foot on Cape Henry in 1607 and established the first permanent English settlement in America.

THE NELSON HOUSE, built around 1711 by Scotch Tom Nelson, of Revolutionary War fame. When the British captured Yorktown and seized the house, Nelson offered a prize to the first soldier to hit it. The ball remains in one wall.

OCTOBER 19, 1981 . . . the bicentennial celebration of Lord Cornwallis' surrender of British forces at Yorktown, virtually ending the Revolutionary War. 180,000 attended the festivities. Photos, counter-clockwise: young member of Continental Fife and Drum Crops with modern warships in York River; the former presidential yacht *Sequoia* seen from Gloucester Point, framed by the stern of *The Dove* and aft deck of a skipjack; the Victory Monument on Main Street, constructed 100 years after the war to commemorate the French and American alliance which led to victory.

95

GLOUCESTER, VIRGINIA . . . gets a fresh topcoat of white to set off its colonial buildings: Long Bridge Ordinary (left page), 1750, used to store arms during the Revolutionary War; Gloucester County Court House, 1766; and Ware Church, raised in 1690, replacing an earlier church. The brick church, with walls three feet thick, is considered an excellent example of a colonial rectangular church. The church has communion silver made in London in 1675 which came indirectly as a gift from Augustine Warner, great-grandfather of George Washington. Gloucester County has more waterfront than any county in Virginia which made it accessible for early development. The first people came here in 1607, but Indian massacres wiped out the settlers in 1620 and 1640. The county was finally established in 1651.

LOBLOLLY PINES are set afire by this October sunset photographed from Fishing Bay Marina, Deltaville.

GWYNN'S ISLAND . . . One of the coldest days of early 1982, the view from old Texaco Wharf on Cricket Hill to Callis Wharf on Gwynn's Island is a mirror of ice. Gwynn's Island is situated at the mouth of the Piankatank River and features the delightful Islander Resort Motel. The next to last land battle of the Revolution was fought here.

HARBOUR HOUSE STUDIO . . . This weatherbeaten old sea house with curvature of the spine is loved by someone in Deltaville.

DEAGLE'S MARINE RAILWAY is a port in the storm for fishing boats in Deltaville, Va. The *Mildred Belle*, an oyster buy boat mentioned in the Pulitzer Prize winning book, *Beautiful Swimmers*, gets some on-board adjustments from her skipper. The boat was built in 1948 and is sound from stem to stern.

PROPELLER that cost $600 to be reconditioned dwarfs the carpenter working on this buy boat at Deagle's Marine Railway, one of 13 boat yards in Deltaville.

OLD SEA CAPTAINS are a delight to talk with, no less David Winegar, 67 (right) whose dad started this marine railway on George's Cove near White Stone, Va. in 1911. Winegar has raised about a dozen raccoons, a few geese and some crows after what seemed like a lifetime aboard submarines and tugboats. "I used to have a crow that would take the clothes pins off the line," he said. "Crows are smart. You never saw one run over on the road." Winegar remembers attending the 150th anniversary of Cornwallis' surrender at Yorktown in 1931 with a girl who lived right across the cove. "She met a French sailor down there, went over to France and married him," he said. "But it didn't work. She came back."

THE BELLS ARE RINGING at the Mathews Baptist Church, organized in 1776, on the middle neck of Tidewater Virginia.

HYCO is the name of this Victorian house in Mathews, Va. which strongly resembles the stature and design of the homes of the menhaden fish captains of the early part of this century. Reedville, across the Rappahannock to the north, is the center of the menhaden industry. In the 1920s the town had the highest per capita income in the U.S. Hyco is more than 100 years old but the original owner is unknown.

THE ALL PURPOSE GARAGE . . . What else could a man want? A fishing boat, pickup truck and load of fire wood are stowed in this Mathews County garage in Dutton, Va.

ROSEGILL . . . On the southern banks of the Rappahannock River, where it is five miles wide, and across the creek from the picture postcard town of Urbanna, sits this majestic plantation house built by Ralph Wormley in 1656. One of the Wormley daughters married Landon Carter, a son of King Carter, the richest and most powerful man in Virginia. It was customary for the families of the land barons to inter-marry. Five generations of Wormleys lived here until 1806, including a colonial governor.

MILL CREEK LANDING . . . Round stern workboats line up on a rare day off on the south shores of the Rappahannock near Urbanna (the Norris Bridge is on the horizon just to the right of the trees).

URBANNA

VIRGINIA STREET

ROAD TO URBANNA CREEK . . . is Virginia Street, which leads past the Urbanna Public Library (left), the old customs house (above) and to crab pots and a beached fishing boat (left page). Across the frozen creek is the Rosegill farm area. Hogsheads of tobacco were rolled down Virginia Street to a wharf in colonial times, hence the former name of Prettyman's Rolling Road. The library is housed in an old warehouse built in 1766. The customs house was built in 1754-62, restored in 1805 and was the home of a governor of Virginia, Andrew Jackson Montague. He named the place *Little Sandwich* after the English home of the Earl of Sandwich, to whom he was related. Robert L. Montague, 3d, Esq., grandson of the governor, lives there now.

AMERICAN EAGLE: MACHO LIFESTYLE

AMERICAN EAGLES mate for life. They carry on in a way to which any human couple can relate. Mother Eagle spends a late winter day sitting on her eggs (left). Old dad spends the day whirling around Urbanna Creek grundging for food. And he's not against a little intimidation. An osprey flies over the huge nest. A few seconds later the bald one is in hot pursuit, gets the fish hawk to drop his fish and goes underneath to snag it for his family. Late in the day Mom yells like a banshee: "Get me off these rocks, I need some relief." Dad arrives a few minutes later and they go off and do a waltz in the sky together (right page) within sight of their eggs. Mom then goes off for a spin of her own while Dad drops onto a sturdy branch alongside the nest.

He refuses to sit on the eggs. After about 15 minutes, his patience evaporated, he lets out a Bronx cheer (above) for his mate to return. She arrives in 10 minutes, drops on her eggs and he resumes his hunt for food. In the early spring Mom has two eaglets which are soon banded by the wildlife officials who climb the 50-foot high loblolly pine tree. As of 1981 there were 94 nesting pairs of bald eagles in the Bay area, including the Urbanna, Va. pair (left) and the pair on the right page from Greenwood Creek, Queen Anne's County, Maryland.

URBANNA CREEK . . . whose high banks in the area above the town bridge make ideal nesting for the American Eagle shown on the preceding pages.

URBANNA BRIDGE, (above) in upper right hand corner, is the cutoff between marinas and moorings and the open gunkholing water on the opposite page. The picturesque middle neck Tidewater town is jammed with up to 25,000 people at its oyster festival the first week of November. Rappahannock River is at bottom left. Historic "Rosegill" is on left side of creek.

TIDES INN (below) was constructed in 1945 across the Rappahannock from Urbanna on lovely Carter's Creek. The Northern Neck resort showplace features a 120-foot Trumpy yacht at the end of its pier which takes hotel guests for an excursion ride every day at noon when the weather is favorable.

ON JANUARY 15, 1982 the little Tidewater Virginia town of Irvington was transformed into a plain of white by its heaviest snow in a dozen years. Appropriately, a Siberian Husky appeared out of nowhere at King Carter Inn (above) and the Irvington United Methodist Church (far right). Carter's Creek, which runs through and around Irvington, is the setting for iced-in workboats and sailboats (above) as seen from the second floor of the Irvington Marina office; and as a tableau for artists (far right). The latter setting is identical to the fall scene on the dust jacket and on page 113. The work boat Marg-Re-Dot cracked out of the ice at 7 A.M. Tides Lodge is in the background.

IRVINGTON, VA.

HISTORIC CHRIST CHURCH, built in 1732 by Robert King Carter, stands between the Northern Neck towns of Irvington and Kilmarnock. It is considered "the most perfect example of colonial church architecture" in Virginia. Carter was a builder and tobacco grower. When he died he was the richest and most powerful man in Virginia. His direct descendants include two presidents (the Harrisons) and General Robert E. Lee. The boxed pews and stone floors are today as they were 250 years ago. King Carter and his two wives, who bore him 12 children, are buried in ornate tombs near the church.

CHRIST CHURCH was in such a state of disrepair after the Civil War that the doors fell off their hinges. A story emanated out of that era concerning a Mrs. Ima Angel, a black lady who lived near the brick building. She was caught in a sudden rainstorm one night and sought temporary shelter so as not to get her white dress dirty. She waited out the storm in King Carter's pew in front of the altar. A man on horseback rode by a few minutes later and also sought shelter. He rode his horse down the stone floor to Carter's pew when he saw what appeared to be a white apparition. "Who is there?" he asked. "Ima Angel," she replied. Scant seconds later Mrs. Angel was alone again in the church.

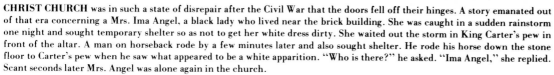

HEAVY FROST lies like a white sheet across the lawn of this simple, white frame Mt. Olive Baptist Church, organized in 1910, in the Middle Neck village of Hartfield, Va.

CARTER'S CREEK in Irvington, Virginia wakes up to
a frosty, misty morning in late October.

OLD SCOT ARMS TAVERN in Tappahannock, Va. is one of the oldest structures in this 300-year-old river town along the Rappahannock. "George Washington never slept here and we haven't had any murders or any ghosts but we do have a sailor buried in the back yard garden who was drowned in 1728 when he fell off a mast of a ship in the river," declared Mary Derieux, whose family has lived in the handsome house behind the white picket fence for 100 years. "He was from Glasgow, Scotland." Records indicate the tavern was built about 1706, but the foundation bears evidence of an earlier date. After its tavern days, the building became a girls school; then a private residence.

GHOST COUNTRY . . . Sabine Hall (left and below) has this reputation for, uh, apparitions. Located near Warsaw on Virginia's Northern Neck, this Greek inspired mansion was built in 1730 by tobacco king Robert (King) Carter for one of his eight sons, Landon. Landon had three wives and his two sons had a total of three wives. The plantation house held a succession of greetings for bride and groom and therein developed the tale that has persisted for generations: when the couple entered the great doorway and ascended the grand staircase, on a landing stood a little page gaily dressed for the occasion. The page greeted the bride with a big welcoming smile, then vanished. All of the brides were to have witnessed this phenomenon.

The stone barn below leads down to the northern shores of the Rappahannock.

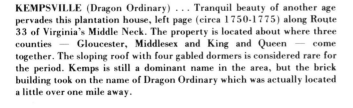

KEMPSVILLE (Dragon Ordinary) . . . Tranquil beauty of another age pervades this plantation house, left page (circa 1750-1775) along Route 33 of Virginia's Middle Neck. The property is located about where three counties — Gloucester, Middlesex and King and Queen — come together. The sloping roof with four gabled dormers is considered rare for the period. Kemps is still a dominant name in the area, but the brick building took on the name of Dragon Ordinary which was actually located a little over one mile away.

STRATFORD HALL stands like a ghost in a January snowstorm, its Great House and dependencies barely visible across the great lawn. This birthplace of the Lee family and, most prominently, Robert E. Lee, has stood for two and one half centuries, including the old slave quarters (middle). Prized cattle are most willing to have their picture taken.

COURT HOUSE SQUARE in the historic little Northern neck town of Montross, Va. shows, in the throes of a very white winter, the old Westmoreland County Court House, 1774; the museum and library (left) and The Inn at Montross (barely visible, rear) which was called John Minor's Ordinary more than 300 years ago. Thomas Lee, great uncle of Robert E. Lee, was a frequent visitor to this inn during his tenure as a burgess. Thomas Lee built Stratford Hall in 1725. Below, Old Jail and Library, circa 1819, in nearby Lancaster, Va.

Below: HAUNTED HOUSE . . .
on Route 3 in Lyells, Va.

Above: **THE EMBERS** . . . replica of an 18th century Tidewater Virginia ordinary, located in a hamlet called Log Cabin just north of Kilmarnock. The building was constructed of old wood from a Confederate warehouse in Richmond. A log cabin called Steptoes Ordinary sat on this perch in the late 1700s. Overnight lodging is still available and guests may warm themselves by the open fireplaces. Below: **POND SHACKS** . . . between Heathsville and Callao on Route 360.

Right Page: **FOLLOW THE LEADER** is the name of the game as steel stemmed oyster boats lead their more vulnerable companions through the ice of the Patuxent at the eastern tip of Solomon's Island.

UPPER WESTERN SHORE

THOMAS JOHNSON MEMORIAL BRIDGE, spanning a frozen Patuxent.

SOLOMONS, MD.

Left Page: **DRUM POINT LIGHTHOUSE,** built in 1883, as she appears today at Calvert Marine Museum, Solomons. There once were 40 cottage type, screw pile lighthouses on the Bay; this is one of the three survivors. The others are Thomas Point at the mouth of the South River, and Hooper's Strait at Chesapeake Bay Maritime Museum, St. Michaels. Right: **OUR LADY STAR OF THE SEA CHURCH,** Solomons Harbor.

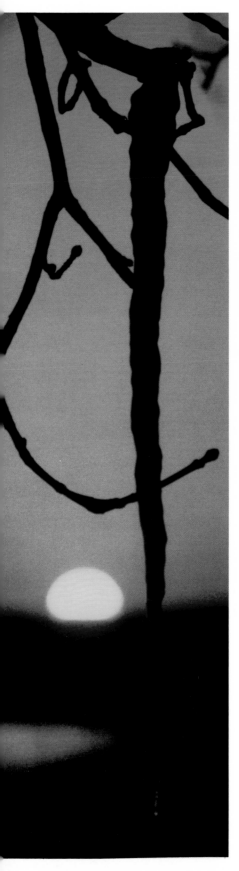

CHAPEL POINT . . . "Sentinels" of the St. Ignatius Church cemetery look down on the confluence of the little Tobacco River and the Potomac, the Chesapeake Bay's largest river which divides Maryland and Virginia. An icicle from a sugar maple tree at the cemetery lends a bit of op-art as the sun sets. St. Ignatius Church was founded in 1641 and is said to be the oldest continually active parish in the U.S., dating from 1662. Father Andrew White, SJ, founded the church and named Chapel Point. Present church (right) was built in 1798.

CHRIST CHURCH AT CHAPTICO, MD. (left) was built in 1736. The steeple was added in 1918. It is believed that the distinguished Sir Christopher Wrenn was the designer. Philip Key, the great-grandfather of Francis Scott Key, is buried in a vault beneath the church. It is said that the rector would delay the service to await the arrival of Philip — who was a member of the General Assembly and Privy Council, and was high sheriff. Nearby Chaptico Landing was one of the busiest ports in Maryland, but sediment filled in the once broad Chaptico Bay.

POTOBAC, an Indian village visited by Capt. John Smith in 1608, became the government and commercial center of Charles County as Port Tobacco. From 1658 to 1895 the little town was the county seat. Port Tobacco River, which flows into the Potomac, served as an important tobacco export point until sediment made it too shallow. Washington visited here frequently, including the chimney house (above and right). The court house (circa 1819) now serves as the Charles County Museum. Old Christ Church sat alongside the court house, but only a marker remains.

WOODSTOCK . . . (above) in southern Prince Georges County. The lower end of the plantation house was built in 1798, the middle in 1820. This is precisely the idyllic scene, with sheep grazing, that one observes driving south towards Waldorf on Route 301.

THE SPORT IS THE SAME (as Salisbury) but not the terrain here in Glyndon, northwest of Baltimore. Sleet fell the morning of this Thanksgiving Day fox hunt. Red foxes were brought over from England and first let loose in Centreville, Md.

AMISH COUNTRY . . : Between the Patuxent River on the east and the Potomac to the west the self sufficient and industrious Amish folk abound. Their windmills, buggies, laundry lines, crisply neat homes and one room school houses are a way of life along roads such as Routes 6 and 236. The Amish market place shown is at Charlotte Hall, Maryland on Route 5.

PLAIN NECESSITY . . . The Amish home is full of plain truths, and no telephones. But an Amish man coming from market in nearby Charlotte Hall, Maryland finds it necessary to make Ma Bell part of his business routine on Route 236 in northeast St. Mary's County.

GODIAH SPRAY PLANTATION . . . A 17th century plantation dwelling house (above) was erected along with two tobacco barns by carpenters in St. Mary's City along the Milburn Creek in the fall of 1981. Nearby, archeologists dug for artifacts to gain knowledge of how people lived in Maryland's first capital in the 1600s. The State of Maryland is paying for the unearthing and reproduction of its origins. Godiah Spray is a fictitious Englishman composite who just got off the boat.

TOBACCO COUNTRY . . . Harvested tobacco leaves air dry in open slat barns in Port Tobacco and Leonardtown (top to bottom). Tobacco served as currency in Maryland for 100 years.

THE CHAPEL at the height of the autumn blaze on the campus of the U.S. Naval Academy, Annapolis.

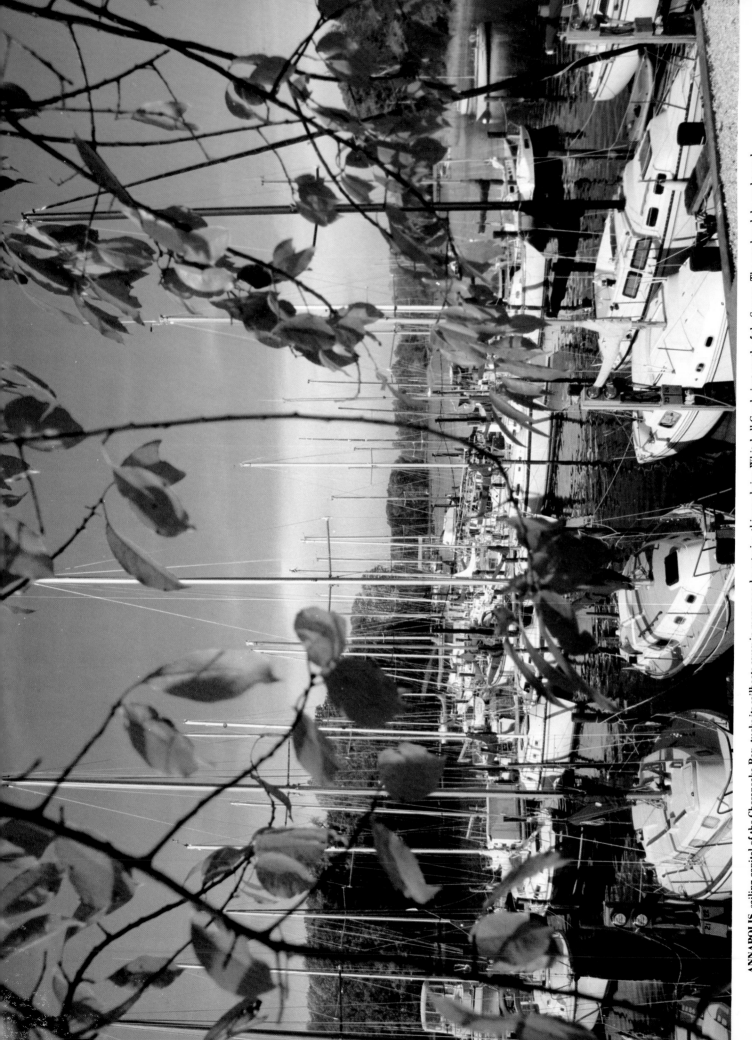

ANNAPOLIS, sailing capital of the Chesapeake Bay, tucks its sailboats away in many nearby arteries, this one being Whitehall Creek, just north of the Severn. The creek and the yacht yard (above) take their name from the famous nearby Whitehall estate, summer home of Horatio Sharpe, one of the early governors of Maryland. The home was built in 1760.

CALM BEFORE THE STORM . . . Early morning scene along City Dock before the crowds flood downtown Annapolis for the annual motorboat show. In the foreground is the After Deck Lounge of The Hilton. Steeples of the old Maryland State House (left) and The Chapel of the U.S. Naval Academy (right) are in clear view on this crystal day.

131

Top: **CITY DOCK . . .** When the weather turns cold and brisk, oyster boats become a familiar sight hauling their catch into the restaurants and sea food houses in downtown Historic Annapolis. Bottom: **BREAKFAST AT THE HILTON . . .** This is the view waiting for you in the fifth floor dining room of The Hilton during the Annapolis Sailboat Show in October, if you care to get up this early for breakfast. The sun rises on the Eastern Shore and casts its glow on the sailboats dug in on Spa Creek, with nary a sailor in sight.

REVOLUTION RETURNS TO ANNAPOLIS

RE-ENACTMENT of the role of Annapolis in Rochambeau's Revolutionary march 200 years ago gave visitors to Maryland's historical capital city on October 14, 1981 an opportunity to view the campuses of the U.S. Naval Academy (left) and St. John's College (right). Costumed colonial militia units did battle with the "British" along College Creek (below) while an academy crew tried to keep beat and watch the action. A "camp follower" and Continental Army soldier engage in conversation (right). Francis Scott Key, author of the National Anthem, was graduated from old St. John's in 1796. He was then 16.

TALL SHIPS IN ANNAPOLIS ... Tall ships such as the sloop *PROVIDENCE* (below and at right) and the clipper ship *PRIDE OF BALTIMORE* (on the horizon) were constructed for America's Bicentennial celebration in 1976. They continue to provide a school of knowledge of our maritime past, serve as ambassadors for their cities in far places and participate in patriotic events such as the transport by sea of militiamen from Annapolis to Yorktown during the Revolutionary War celebrations in 1981. Past the aft deck of the *PROVIDENCE* may be observed U.S. Naval Academy ships training on the Severn. Twelve "colonial troops" slept on deck of the *PROVIDENCE* on the October 15 trip down the Chesapeake. The *PROVIDENCE* is a replica of the Revolutionary War sloop that captured 40 British ships. The horizon photograph of the *PRIDE* was taken at a distance of at least a mile. She took the anchored coal ship on her port and Thomas Point Lighthouse (right page) on her starboard. The picture of the Bay's most photographed lighthouse, at the mouth of the South River and automated in 1981, was taken on February 28, 1982 after a two-inch snowfall.

WINTER LOCKS IN ANNAPOLIS CITY DOCK and a log brogan sailboat named *MUSTANG* (extreme left), built in 1907. It is the last five log brogan under sail. It was entered on the national Register of Historic Places in 1981. At far right is the Chart House Restaurant across Spa Creek, once the construction barn for the elegant Trumpy yachts.

CURTIS CREEK . . . There is a certain esthetic quality to the A. Smith and Sons Shipyard just off the Patapsco River in Baltimore. The red tugboats, the blue water and a 1923 Trumpy named *Ebenezer II* make it come alive. The Trumpy, restored here by former New Jersey tennis champion Jim Orange and his wife Carol, embarked for Fort Lauderdale soon after this photo was made. The 72-foot wooden classic served as an excursion boat there. One of its customers was a 28-year-old Saudi Arabian sheik who paid up to $600 an hour to take his entourage for a boat ride. Across Curtis Creek is the **W. R. Grace Co.** plant which manufactures tooth paste, fuel oil additives, etc.

CONSTELLATION, oldest ship in the U.S. Navy, seen from the 25th floor of the World Trade Center, Baltimore Inner Harbor, and in a "ground floor" snow storm. The Constellation was launched September 7, 1797 from Fells Point and never lost a battle in 160 years of service. Harborplace serves as the background for both photographs.

FORMER PRESIDENTIAL YACHT, *SEQUOIA*, privately owned since 1977, rests in an Inner Harbor winter wonderland of snow-crowned paddle boats, and silhouetted sailboats. A misty National Aquarium is in the background. The mahogany and fir planked yacht was built in 1924 by the Mathis Boat Co. John Trumpy designed her. She acquired her name when purchased by the Sequoia Petroleum Co., of Texas. Eight presidents used the 104-foot vessel since 1933. Herbert Hoover liked to toss a medicine ball on deck,

FDR entertained Winston Churchill aboard her during World War II. Kennedy celebrated his 46th birthday within its panelled accommodations and Nixon told his family of his plans to resign the Presidency while cruising the Potomac during the Watergate summer of '74. Carter, a former Navy man, saw no entertainment in her $800,000 annual maintenance cost, and had her sold. She has had four owners since Carter pulled anchor.

INNER HARBOR: AUTUMN

BALTIMORE INNER HARBOR in the autumn, cool and uncrowded. Centers of interest are, clockwise, Harborplace mall (left); World Trade Center, which is the tallest pentagonal building in the United States; the one-year-old National Aquarium and its outdoor seal pool (above). Below, Fells Point to the starboard as one would arrive at the Inner Harbor by boat. William Fell, a shipbuilder from Lancashire, England, established Fells Point in 1726. More than 600 ships were built in the maritime community from the colonial period through the Civil War. This was the birthplace of America's oldest warship, the frigate Constellation, and the home of the swift clipper ships used during the War of 1812. Fells Point is being restored in the architecture of its past.

INTO THE WILD BLUE YONDER . . . Loch Raven Reservoir serves as an ideal place to observe the Baltimore skyline through icy branches on a frigid afternoon, or to watch a couple ice skate into the horizon.

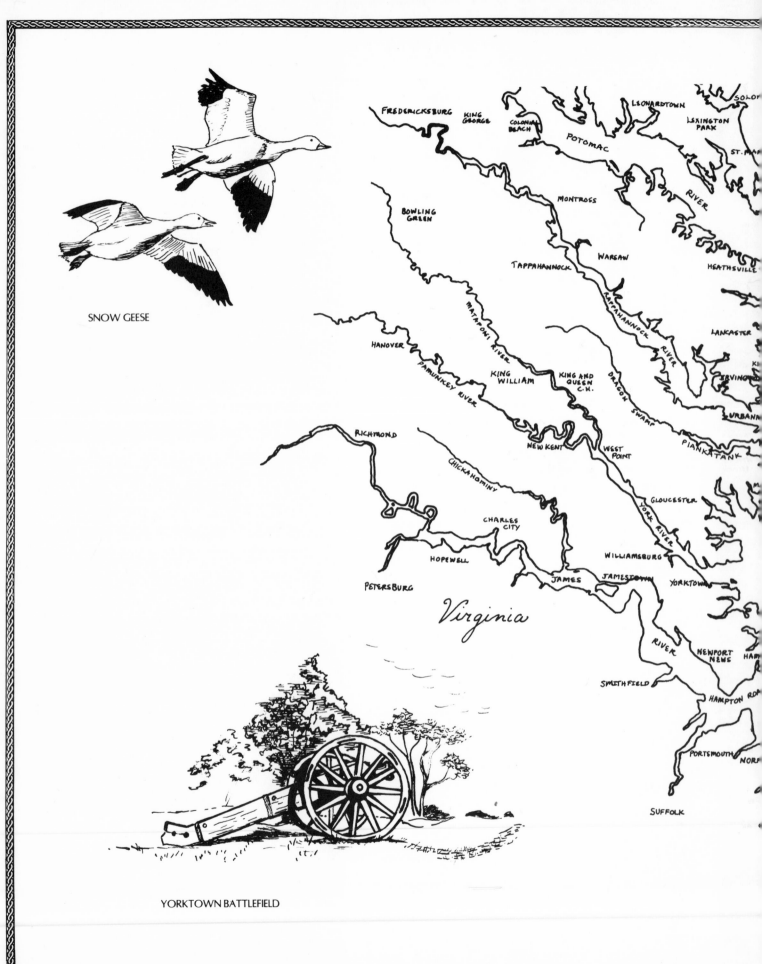

SNOW GEESE

FREDERICKSBURG KING GEORGE COLONIAL BEACH

LEONARDTOWN SOLOM

LEXINGTON PARK

POTOMAC

ST. MAR

BOWLING GREEN

MONTROSS

RIVER

WARSAW

TAPPAHANNOCK

HEATHSVILLE

MATAPONI RIVER

RAPPAHANNOCK RIVER

LANCASTER

HANOVER

PAMUNKEY RIVER

KING WILLIAM

KING AND QUEEN C.H.

DRAGON SWAMP

IRVINGTON

URBANN

PIANKATANK

RICHMOND

CHICKAHOMINY

NEW KENT

WEST POINT

GLOUCESTER

YORK RIVER

CHARLES CITY

HOPEWELL

WILLIAMSBURG

JAMESTOWN

YORKTOWN

PETERSBURG

JAMES

Virginia

RIVER

NEWPORT NEWS

HAM

SMITHFIELD

HAMPTON ROA

PORTSMOUTH NORF

SUFFOLK

YORKTOWN BATTLEFIELD